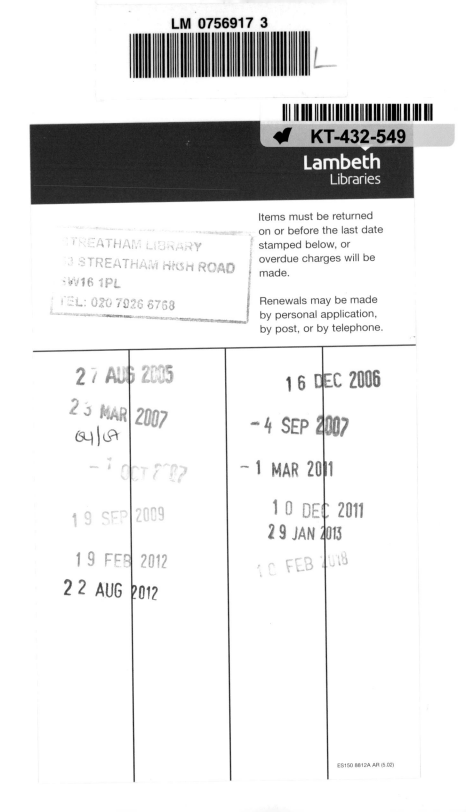

world tour
China

NOELLE MORRIS

www.raintreepublishers.co.uk
Visit our website to find out more information about Raintree books.

To order:
- ☎ Phone 44 (0) 1865 888112
- 🖹 Send a fax to 44 (0) 1865 314091
- 💻 Visit the Raintree Bookshop at **www.raintreepublishers.co.uk** to browse our catalogue and order online.

First published in Great Britain by Raintree Publishers, Halley Court, Jordan Hill, Oxford, OX2 8EJ, part of Harcourt Education.
Raintree is a registered trademark of Harcourt Education Ltd.

Editorial: Sally Knowles
Cover Design: Peter Bailey and Michelle Lisseter
Production: Jonathan Smith

Printed and bound in China and Hong Kong by South China Printing Company

ISBN 1 844 21303 X
07 06 05 04 03
10 9 8 7 6 5 4 3 2 1

British Library Cataloguing in Publication Data
Morris, Noelle
China. - (World tour)
951
A full catalogue for this book is available from the British Library

Acknowledgements
The publishers would like to thank the following for permission to reproduce photographs
p. **1a** ©Susan Lapides; p. **1b** ©Picture Finders Ltd/Leo de Wys Photo Agency; p. **1c** ©Steve Vidler/Leo de Wys Photo Agency; p. **3a** ©Picture Finders Ltd/Leo de Wys Photo Agency; p. **3b** ©Steve Vidler/Leo de Wys Photo Agency; p. **5a** ©Christopher Liu/ChinaStock; p. **5b** ©Christohper Liu/ChinaStock; p. **6** ©Pictor; p. **7** ©Keren Su/Pacific Stock; p. **8** ©Bettmann/CORBIS; p. **13a** ©Bill Bachman/eStock; p. **13b** ©IFA Bilderteam/eStock; p. **14** ©Art Directors; p. **15b** ©Darrell Gulin/DRK Photo; p. **16** ©Liaison/Getty Images; p. **17** ©Dean Conger/CORBIS; p. **20** ©Steve Vidler/Leo de Wys Photo Agency; p. **21** ©SuperStock; p. **23** ©Joe Carini Pacific Stock; p. **25a** ©DRK Photo; p. **27a** ©Pierre Colombel/CORBIS; p. **27b** ©Julia Waterlow/Eye Ubiquitous/CORBIS; p. **28** ©Forrest Anderson/TimePix; p. **29** ©Rob Tringali Jr./SportsChrome; p. **31b** ©Liaison/Getty Images; p. **33** ©Dennis Cox/ChinaStock; p. **34** ©Eric Futran/FoodPix; p. **35b** ©Dennis Cox/ ChinaStock; p. **35a** ©Sovfoto/Eastfoto, p. **37** ©AFP/CORBIS; p. **38b** ©Keren Su/CORBIS; p. **40** ©Keren Su/Pacific Stock; p. **41** ©Bill Bachmann/eStock; p. **42** ©Liaison/Getty Images; p. **43c** ©Todd Gipstein/CORBIS; p. **43b** ©Wolfgang Kaehler/CORBIS; p. **44a** ©Mansell/TimePix; p. **44b** ©Eye Ubiquitous/Geof Daniels, p. **44c** ©winston fraser

Additional photography by PhotoDisc and Steck-Vaughn Collection.

Cover photographs: Getty Images/Imagebank/Keren Su

Contents

Welcome to China

Whether you are planning to travel or want to find out about other **cultures** and people, China is a country with a colourful past, breathtaking sites and more than a thousand million people. There is plenty for visitors to see and do.

Pronunciation guide

Xia   (SHE'ah)

Qin   (CHEE-in)

Qing   (CHEE-ing)

Deng Xiaoping   (DENNG-SHE'ow-PING)

Yangtze   (YANG-ZHAY)

Beijing   (BAY-ZHING)

Tiananmen   (TEE-eh-NAH-men)

Shih Huang-ti   (SHIH-HWONG'tee)

Xian   (SHE'ahn)

Taiyung   (TIE-yoong)

Yinchuan   (YIN-CHU'ahn)

Jiang Zemin   (ZHE'ahng-ZAY-MIN)

▶ **MOON FESTIVAL**
A family shares a tray of moon cakes to celebrate the Moon Festival in autumn.

▲ **DANCING WITH DRAGONS**
The Dragon Dance is a highlight of Chinese New Year celebrations. In Chinese culture, dragons are considered to be friendly, helpful creatures.

China's past

It is helpful for visitors to learn a little about China's past before going there. Through the centuries, many different families of kings and emperors ruled China. These ruling families were called **dynasties**. Each dynasty played a part in making the China of today.

Dynasties

It is believed that the first dynasty in China was the Xia, or Hsia, Dynasty and that it ruled from 2200 to 1766 BC. It is thought that the people made beautiful pottery and developed a writing system. In about 1000 BC the Chou Dynasty created the first **bureaucracy**. Confucius was alive then. His philosophical writings are world famous.

The first emperor of China belonged to the Qin, or Ch'in, Dynasty and he united China. The Qin Dynasty ruled China from 221 to 206 BC and is remembered for beginning the Great Wall of China. In those days it was built of soil and stone.

◀ **FORBIDDEN CITY, BEIJING**
Ming Dynasty rulers built the Forbidden City. Called Gu Gong in Chinese, the Forbidden City was the home of China's emperors from 1420 to 1911. It is the largest palace complex in the world.

▲ **LESHAN GIANT BUDDHA**
Near Leshan in central China, the largest stone Buddha in the world stands 71 metres high.

The next great Chinese dynasty was the Han which ruled from 202 BC to AD 220. The Han emperors made a model of government based on the teachings of Confucius. Today, the largest **ethnic group** in China is called the Han.

The T'ang Dynasty followed the Han. It lasted from 618 to 907. The T'ang expanded China's borders in all directions. Empress Wu was a ruler during this period. She deposed her son as emperor, exiled him and then installed her second son as emperor and ruled with him.

The Ming Dynasty came next and ruled from 1368 to 1644. This family was brutal – one emperor beheaded more than 40,000 people for one crime. The Ming became a great **naval** power. A man named Zheng led an expedition of 300 Chinese ships to Africa.

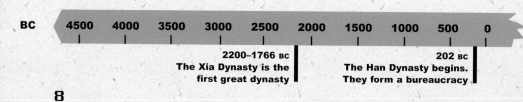

▲ CHAIRMAN MAO
Mao Zedong was China's most important political leader of the 20th century. Mao ruled China from 1949 to 1976. He was chairman of the Chinese Communist Party.

Recent history

The Manchus invaded China in 1644 and began the Qing dynasty. They ruled until 1911. Under their rule, Chinese culture blossomed. The Qing emperors adopted a new Chinese 'world view' and **isolated** themselves from the rest of the world. However, isolation became hard by the time World War I erupted in 1914.

BC 4500 4000 3500 3000 2500 2000 1500 1000 500 0

2200–1766 BC
The Xia Dynasty is the
first great dynasty

202 BC
The Han Dynasty begins.
They form a bureaucracy

The Chinese government sided with the **Allies** in World War I but the land China thought would be theirs after the war was given to Japan instead. In 1937, Japan invaded China and the Japanese army committed many **atrocities** against the Chinese people. Millions of people died by the time World War II ended in 1945.

The People's Republic of China

In 1949, China's new **Communist** government was established. Its leader, Chairman Mao Zedong, declared the birth of the People's Republic of China which became a world power. In 1958, China began to break its ties with the Soviet Union. Chairman Mao started a programme called the Great Leap Forward to improve Chinese industry, but the programme failed. There was a severe famine, and millions of people starved to death.

In 1966, China was in **turmoil**. Chairman Mao launched the Great **Proletarian** Cultural **Revolution**. The upheaval of this revolution lasted until Mao's death in 1976. In 1978, Deng Xiaoping became leader. He began a series of **reforms** which have increased China's economic importance. The Chinese economy is one of the fastest growing in the world.

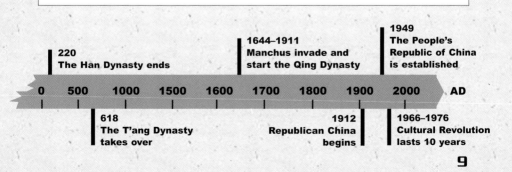

220
The Han Dynasty ends

1644–1911
Manchus invade and
start the Qing Dynasty

1949
The People's
Republic of China
is established

0   500   1000   1500   1600   1700   1800   1900   2000   AD

618
The T'ang Dynasty
takes over

1912
Republican China
begins

1966–1976
Cultural Revolution
lasts 10 years

9

A look at China's geography

China is a large country located in eastern Asia. Russia, Canada and the USA are the only countries in the world that are larger than China.

Land

China makes up almost 7 per cent of the Earth's land mass. That is a large amount of land, especially when you consider that almost 70 per cent of the Earth's surface is covered in water.

The world's tallest mountain, Mount Everest, is located on the border between China and Nepal. Mount Everest is 8850 metres high – almost 9 kilometres (5.5 miles) and it is one of the most challenging mountains in the world to climb. China also has two huge deserts, the Taklimakan Desert and the Gobi Desert. The Taklimakan is an enormous desert which measures 272,000 square kilometres (105,000 square miles). Its name means 'Place of No Return'. It is covered with sand dunes and rocky soil. The Gobi Desert also has rocky and sandy soil. It is the second-largest desert in the world and occupies 1,295,000 square kilometres (500,000 square miles). Only the Sahara Desert in Africa is bigger.

▶ CHINA'S SIZE

The People's Republic of China covers an area of 9,596,960 sq km (3,705,392 sq miles) – nearly 40 times bigger than the UK. Two-thirds of China is made up of mountains and deserts.

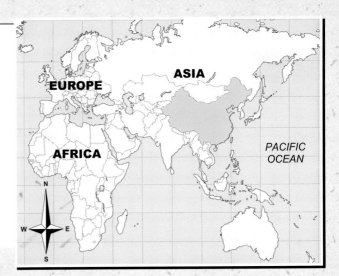

CHINA

★ National capital
● Major city

| 0 | 300 | 600 Kilometres |
| 0 | 300 | 600 Miles |

RUSSIA

KAZAKHSTAN

MONGOLIA

N. KOREA

KYRGYZSTAN   Gobi Desert   Beijing ★

S. KOREA

TAJIKISTAN   Taklimakan
Desert   Great Wall of China

JAPAN

●Shanghai

PAKISTAN   C H I N A

NEPAL   Taipei ●

BHUTAN   Taiwan

INDIA   PACIFIC
                                                  OCEAN
BANGLADESH   Hong Kong ●

MYANMAR   VIETNAM

LAOS

Water

Water plays an important role in China's geography. Three major bodies of water border the eastern coast of China. The Yellow Sea lies along the north-eastern coast, the East China Sea is in the east and the South China Sea lies along the south-east coast.

China also has several major rivers. The Chang Jiang and Huang He are China's two main freshwater sources. The Chang Jiang is also called the Yangtze and the Huang He is also known as the Yellow River. Both of these rivers provide water for the eastern half of China. The water keeps the land quite **fertile**, making it some of the best farmland in the world.

Reader's tip: You have read about the land in China. Can you find the places mentioned here on the map?

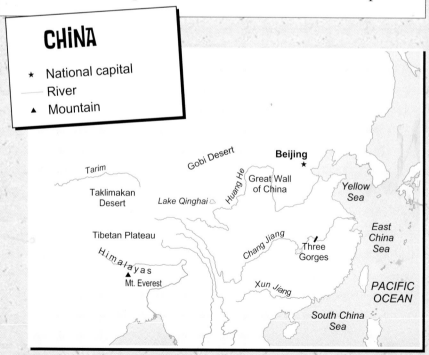

CHINA

★ National capital
— River
▲ Mountain

Tarim

Gobi Desert

Beijing ★

Taklimakan Desert

Lake Qinghai △

Huang He

Great Wall of China

Yellow Sea

Tibetan Plateau

East China Sea

Chang Jiang

Three Gorges

Himalayas

▲ Mt. Everest

Xun Jiang

PACIFIC OCEAN

South China Sea

▲ **RICE PADDIES**
Rice is grown in paddies, small fields flooded with water. Most of China's rice is grown in the southern part of the country. Wheat grows in the north.

▶ **PRECIOUS HARVESTS**
Only about 13 per cent of China's land is suitable for growing crops. Throughout its history, China has had to use every bit of land to feed its huge population.

◀ SUMMER RAINS
South-eastern
China gets the
most rainfall, while
the north-west is
driest. Most of the
rain falls in the
summer and the
amount can vary a
lot from year to
year.

Climate

China is a huge country. It has empty deserts, rich farmland and tall mountains. The weather differs from region to region. China lies in the northern **temperate zone** of the Earth so there are four seasons – spring, summer, autumn and winter.

The climate in China is affected by **monsoons**. Monsoons are strong winds that blow across the Indian Ocean and southern Asia. From September to April, the winds cause the air to be dry and cold. In the summer, monsoons come from the ocean. They bring warmer weather and heavy rain. Visitors to China should pack a warm jacket for winter and a light raincoat for summer and it is a good idea to check the weather forecast before going out.

▲ SINGING SANDS

The Taklimakan Desert in north-west China is made up of huge shifting sand dunes. Long ago, silk traders who crossed the desert said the shifting sands made a singing sound that tried to lure them away from their travelling companions and supplies.

Beijing: snapshot of a big city

▲ **THE NORTHERN CAPITAL**
Beijing's tall, modern buildings are topped with traditional-
style Chinese roofs.

The best place to start a visit to Chima is Beijing. It is the capital city of China, with a population of more than 12 million people. It has a famous zoo, beautiful parks and ancient temples, so Beijing has something to interest everyone.

City facts
Beijing is the largest city in China after Shanghai. It is located in northern China, and is 16,835 square kilometres (6500 square miles) in area. For many years, the city was known as Peking which means 'northern capital'.

The Beijing Zoo
The Beijing Zoo is known around the world because of its giant pandas. Only about 1000 giant pandas remain in the wild. They are found only in China. Giant pandas are **endangered**. Much of their natural **habitat** is gone because people have used it for farms and the bamboo they eat has been cut down to be used as scaffolding. Giant pandas do not have enough babies to increase their numbers quickly.

▶ **BEIJING ZOO'S PANDAS**
Playful giant pandas in the Beijing Zoo are one of China's most popular tourist attractions. To many, the giant panda is seen as a symbol of China.

The Forbidden City

This part of Beijing is called the Forbidden City because for many years ordinary people were forbidden to enter. It was built more than 500 years ago and more than 200,000 men were needed to build its walls. It was built as a palace for the emperor but even he was not allowed to enter certain parts of the city.

Today, the city is no longer forbidden. It has ancient ruins and many museums full of treasures that visitors can go and see.

Tiananmen Square

The entrance to Tiananmen Square is fantastic. It has two marble columns decorated with twisting dragons and clouds. Dragons are **symbols** of Chinese culture.

Tiananmen Square is a modern landscape of amazing architecture. It is in what used to be the Forbidden City. Today, it is a place for large celebrations. Every evening, at about seven o'clock, people gather here. They watch the lowering of the Chinese flag opposite the Gate of Tiananmen, which means 'Heavenly Peace'. This is a popular event and people go there early to queue for a seat. Tiananmen Square became famous in 1989 when a huge crowd gathered there to demonstrate for human rights. Some protesters were killed by the army.

▶ TIANANMEN SQUARE

Tiananmen Square was once the site of government buildings within the Forbidden City. The building at the rear of this photo is the Mao Mausoleum. It is where the body of Mao Zedong is kept.

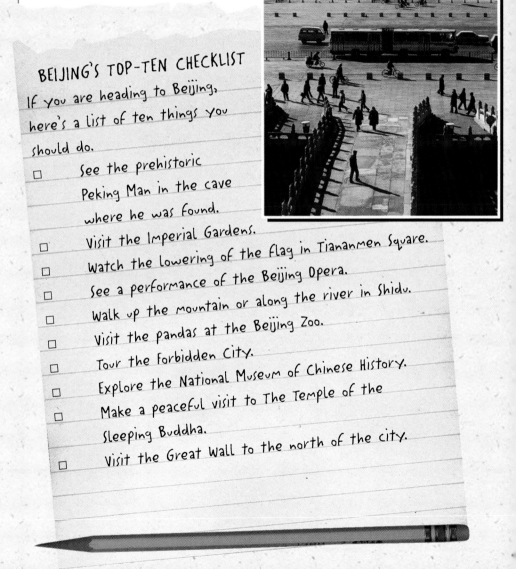

BEIJING'S TOP-TEN CHECKLIST

If you are heading to Beijing, here's a list of ten things you should do.

- ☐ See the prehistoric Peking Man in the cave where he was found.
- ☐ Visit the Imperial Gardens.
- ☐ Watch the lowering of the flag in Tiananmen Square.
- ☐ See a performance of the Beijing Opera.
- ☐ Walk up the mountain or along the river in Shidu.
- ☐ Visit the pandas at the Beijing Zoo.
- ☐ Tour the Forbidden City.
- ☐ Explore the National Museum of Chinese History.
- ☐ Make a peaceful visit to The Temple of the Sleeping Buddha.
- ☐ Visit the Great Wall to the north of the city.

Four top sights

The Great Wall

Visitors to China should try to see the Great Wall. Made of earth, brick and stone, the Great Wall of China is 7300 kilometres (4500 miles) long and more than 2000 years old. It is one of the great wonders of the world. Originally, it was built to keep out enemies but today people come from all over the world to visit it. The Great Wall represents China's will and motivation.

Work began on the Great Wall in the 7th century BC and the first section was completed in 221 BC. Most of the Great Wall that you can see today is the result of work done during the reign of Hung-chih (1487–1505). To support China's new tourism industry, the Great Wall was **renovated** during the 20th century. In 1987, 80 kilometres (50 miles) were opened for tourists near Beijing.

The climb to the top is steep, but it is well worth it because the view from the top of the Great Wall is breathtaking.

▲ **A GREAT WALL...**
An early plan for the Great Wall of China called for 'a beacon every 5 li, a tower every 10 li, a fort every 30 li, and a castle every 100 li'. A li is a Chinese unit of measurement equal to about 500 metres.

▲ ...AND A GREAT CLIMB
Every visitor to China should try to walk a section of the Great Wall. For the ancient Chinese, the wall marked the barrier between the civilized 'Middle Kingdom' of China and the barbarian lands to the north.

The clay men at Ch'in Tomb

Shih Huang-ti was the first emperor of China. He died in 210 BC. and is buried in the Ch'in Tomb in the city of Xian.

This spot is extremely famous because more than 7500 clay warriors guard this ancient tomb, each one carefully moulded in painstaking detail. The statues are made of terracotta, a type of clay. They were discovered during an **excavation**. The archaeologists who dug them up were amazed by the huge numbers of the clay soldiers. Shih Huang-ti's tomb became an instant tourist attraction. It has been more than 2200 years since they were built, yet the clay men at the Ch'in Tomb still stand guard.

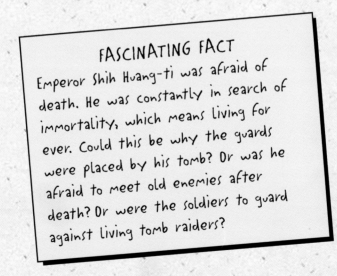

FASCINATING FACT

Emperor Shih Huang-ti was afraid of death. He was constantly in search of immortality, which means living for ever. Could this be why the guards were placed by his tomb? Or was he afraid to meet old enemies after death? Or were the soldiers to guard against living tomb raiders?

▲ A CLAY ARMY
Archaeologists unearthed this ancient army of clay warriors in 1974. They protected the tomb of Emperor Shih Huang-ti. The emperor ordered work to begin on his tomb when he was just thirteen years old.

Hong Kong

Hong Kong is a big city filled with bright lights. In fact, it has one of the largest and most beautiful skylines in Asia. In 1898, Great Britain and China signed a **treaty** allowing Great Britain to **lease** Hong Kong for 99 years which means Great Britain controlled it until 1 July 1997. Today, the wealthy port city is back under Chinese rule.

A first stop in Hong Kong should be Kowloon. There is a lot for visitors to do and excellent hotels, shops and restaurants to visit. Some other popular attractions are the Hong Kong Cultural Centre, the Space Museum and the Museum of History.

Another tourist favourite is Hong Kong Island. It has modern markets, ancient temples and sunny beaches. The ancient Man Mo Temple is especially fascinating. Stanley Market is a popular place for shopping where you can find all sorts of clothing and footwear. The island's most popular beach, Repulse Bay, is a great place to relax.

Hong Kong Island is steep. If you take a ride up the 800-metre escalator, do not look down if you do not like heights. However, if you like being high up, take a trip to Victoria Peak. It rises 552 metres above sea level. The view over Hong Kong is breathtaking.

Readers Tip: Use the map on page 11 to find Hong Kong.

▲ SWEET SMELL OF SUCCESS
Hong Kong means 'Fragrant Harbour', In Chinese. Hong Kong's superb harbour made it a natural site for a port city. Today, it is one of the world's great trade and financial centres.

◀ THE ABACUS
Ancestor of the calculator and the computer, the abacus is used to count and calculate. It is still used in some parts of China and Japan.

The Huang He – the Yellow River

Walking along the Huang He is a good way to experience the Chinese landscape and gives a great view of the mountains. There are ancient caves to explore and untouched grasslands to admire. A boat trip down the river passes several important cities, such as Datong, Taiyung, Hohhot, Baotou, Yinchuan and Lanzhou.

The first stop is Datong and the Yungang Caves. Visitors should explore these huge and ancient caves where there are some amazing statues. The biggest stand more than 17 metres high and others are barely 2 centimetres tall. Datong is also home to the Hanging Monastery, which is an architectural wonder. The monastery is set against a huge rock and supported by poles.

The next stop on the river tour is Hohhot, a large city on the edge of Mongolia. It has a vast grassland area and many historic religious buildings that are hundreds of years old. One of these is the Five Pagoda Temple which was built in the 18th century.

The final stop is Lanzhou which is one of the poorest regions in China. Even so, it is well worth a visit. Lanzhou is home to much of China's industry and scientific research. The White Pagoda Hill has the best view of the city.

▲ ANCIENT CARVINGS
These Buddhist rock temples were carved from the sandstone mountains in the 5th century. They are located at Yungang, near the city of Datong in north-east China.

▶ YELLOW RIVER
The Huang He is called the Yellow River in English. Fine rock and sand carried by the river colour the water and give the river its name.

Going to school in China

Education is very important in China. Over 80 per cent of the population is literate – they are able to read and write. In China, children begin primary school at the age of six or seven and attend school for nine years. Students in China study many of the same subjects as in the United Kingdom. Chinese students go to school six days a week and the school day is long so they do not have very much free time.

Due to China's large population, the classrooms are often crowded. There is not enough room in the universities for everyone who wants a higher education so trying to get a place at university is very competitive.

▲ A CHINESE CLASSROOM
Chinese students go to school six days a week. Classes are taught in one of two Chinese languages – Mandarin or Cantonese.

Chinese sports

Some of the most popular Chinese sports are football, diving, gymnastics and table tennis. The women's football team is world famous and China's divers regularly win medals. The team is regarded as one of the best in the world.

Table tennis is a very widely-played sport in China. It requires a sharp eye and a quick hand. In 1953, players from Asia started to do very well at table tennis and soon began to dominate the sport. They introduced and perfected the 'penholder' grip. This grip is a special way to hold the table-tennis bat and it is now used by many international players.

◀ GYMNASTICS
Gymnast Liu Xuan won a gold medal on the beam at the 2000 Olympic Games. In recent years, China's national gymnastic teams have excelled in international competitions.

From farming to factories

Agriculture in China is of two types. One is farm produce, such as vegetables and the other is saltwater or freshwater fish that are raised in fisheries. China's farmland is very rich, but only 13 per cent of the land can be used for farming because the rest is mountain and desert. Almost 50 per cent of all Chinese people work as farmers – that is a huge number of people working on a small amount of land. While farmers in the West have many technological advances to help them, most farming in China is done the old-fashioned way, using human and animal energy.

Most farmland yields just one crop per year but some land can produce two or three crops. The most important are grains, such as rice and wheat. Other crops, including potatoes and peanuts, are also important to the Chinese economy.

People who live in Beijing, Shanghai or Liaoning, three of the leading industrial cities, do not have to look for a flat to live in because one is assigned to them, close to the factory where they work. China's industry is growing fast. Its main products are textiles, steel and fertilizer. There is also a large mineral resource bank of iron ore. Today's global market and international laws on trade have allowed China to sell lots of its goods to other countries and become a worldwide competitor. With so many resources, China's **economy** promises to continue booming.

▶ HARD WORK

In the rice paddies of southern China, most of the work is still done the traditional way, by hand, without modern machines.

▼ CLOTHING FACTORY

Below, Chinese factory workers sew clothing that is sold around the world. Most factories are found along the east coast, particularly in and around the city of Shanghai.

The Chinese government

China has had a communist government for more than 50 years. Under communism, the government owns all the land, houses and factories and the profits from these are for everyone to share. The government sees its purpose as taking care of all the people.

China is divided into 23 **provinces**. The head of the government is known as the premier. There is also a president, vice president, congress and judicial system. The current president of China is called Jiang Zemin.

China is a **republic**. That means the people elect their rulers, but in China there is only one political party. It is the Communist Party and it controls all of the elections.

For many years, Chinese rulers took an isolationist outlook on world affairs and wanted to keep China separate. Now, like almost everywhere else, the Internet has affected China. It allows people to connect with others all over the world. Some say the Internet is helping Chinese leaders rethink isolationism.

CHINA'S NATIONAL FLAG

The red symbolizes revolution. The five stars stand for the unity of the Chinese people under the Chinese Communist Party. The yellow represents light.

Religions of China

People in China practise many different religions. The most widely spread religions are Buddhism, Taoism and Confucianism. Buddhism is the country's most popular religion and was introduced to China by people from neighbouring India. A key Buddhist belief is that knowledge is important. Trying to learn more and become enlightened is the goal. Taoism teaches certain laws of the universe. The word tao means 'way', 'road' or 'path'. Taoists follow this path to achieve harmony with the universe. Confucianism is a way of life based on the teachings of a **philosopher** called Confucius who lived about 2500 years ago.

Some other people in China practise Christianity and Islam. Christians follow the teachings of Jesus which are found in the New Testament of the Bible. People who practise Islam are called Muslims. They observe the teachings of Mohammed that are written in the Koran.

▶ BUDDHIST MONKS
Buddhist monks hold a service in their temple. In China today there are many Buddhist temples. Buddhist monks and nuns maintain temple services.

Chinese food

Visitors to China should try to eat some local dishes. Chinese food is often eaten out of bowls using chopsticks. You hold these long, thin sticks in one hand and use them to pick up food. People often find this a little tricky to begin with.

Rice and noodles are served at almost every meal. Rice is popular because it grows so well in China. Most meals are prepared in a wok, a special kind of frying pan. The Chinese stir-fry lots of their dishes in the wok. They use many different kinds of vegetables, like bamboo shoots, water chestnuts, mushrooms and bean sprouts.

Dim sum are very popular in China. Dim sum means 'small eats'. Each region has its own version of dim sum. Hong Kong boasts the most famous dim sum chefs. In restaurants, dim sum is not ordered from a menu. Instead, you choose your food, bit by bit, from a trolley pushed around the restaurant. Going out for dim sum is a fun social experience.

◀ **DIM SUM**
These 'small eats' are popular in Hong Kong and throughout south-east China. Dim sum are small portions of tasty foods that are often shared.

MOON CAKES

INGREDIENTS:
570 g flour
340 g butter
500 ml water
2 tsp sugar
pinch salt
450 g sweet red bean paste

WARNING:
**Never cook or bake by yourself.
Always ask an adult to help you
in the kitchen.**

DIRECTIONS:
**Preheat the oven to 200° C or gas
mark 6. Grease a baking sheet.**

**Sift the flour. Put half the flour into
a bowl and mix in half of the butter.
Knead until smooth. Add the rest of
the flour and butter and repeat the
process. Add the water, sugar and salt. Knead the mixture
together. Roll out the dough using a rolling pin. Use a 5-
centimetre pastry cutter to cut
the dough into circles. Bake until
fluffy, then remove from the oven.
Allow the cakes to cool. Spread bean paste
on one cake and place another one on top. Do
this with all the cakes.**

Up close: the Three Gorges Dam

The Three Gorges Dam is being built along the river Chang Jiang (or Yangtze) in Sandouping in eastern China. It is a very controversial project, which means that people are arguing about whether it is right. A dam is a barrier built across the width of a river which stops the water flowing freely.

The project

Completing the Three Gorges Dam is very important to Chinese **commerce**. It will make the water deeper, allowing larger ships to enter the river. Bigger boats mean more trade and more business. More business brings in more jobs and more money.

There are two other major benefits of building this dam. It will protect people from terrible floods. More than 300,000 people have died from floods in the past century. The other benefit is that the dam will use the river water to make electricity. This kind of electricity is called hydroelectricity.

The problem

Even though the dam offers many benefits, it will also do a lot of harm. China's leaders started thinking about building the Three Gorges Dam 80 years ago. Since then, people have argued that it should not be built, saying that the Three Gorges Dam will not only harm the natural environment, it will also affect many people's lives. Work began on the dam in 1955.

▲ THE RIVER

Chang Jiang means 'long river'. The Chang Jiang river is the longest river in China and the third-longest in the world. The proposed Three Gorges Dam will stand more than 180 metres tall and 2 kilometres (1.3 miles) wide.

◀ WHITE CRANE
The Three Gorges Dam project threatens wildlife along the Chang Jiang, including the white crane. In Chinese culture, the white crane is a sacred bird that stands for long life and wisdom.

▲ A MODEL PROJECT?
Onlookers examine a model of the Three Gorges Dam. It is the largest hydroelectric project in history. Once completed, it will be one of three structures made by people that is visible from outer space. The Great Wall of China is another.

Once the dam is completed, 1.5 million people could be forced to move out of their homes. They will have to find new places to live.

Some of the most endangered species in the world could become **extinct** because of the effects of the dam. One such animal is the rare whitefin dolphin. The Chinese sturgeon, a rare type of fish, is also likely to become extinct.

The Three Gorges Dam will cause serious water **pollution** as well. Wastes dumped into the river are washed away quickly. The dam would actually hold the pollution in place. Most people will not think that makes for good drinking water.

More than 1000 important archaeological sites will be destroyed by the dam. In one of these sites, a prehistoric man was discovered. Some scientists believe his bones provide a key to the 'missing link' between humans and animals. This has global importance. It tells us how and where the first humans evolved.

The decision

The Three Gorges Dam is very important, and there are advantages and disadvantages to going ahead. China's government wants to build the dam, and has put many people who protested against it in prison. So what will the final outcome be? We will have to wait until the dam is completed in 2009 to find out.

Holidays

China has three major public holidays – the Chinese New Year, the Dragon Boat Festival, and the Chinese Moon Festival. These holidays are celebrated with parades and fireworks. The Chinese invented fireworks.

Chinese New Year is the most popular holiday. It is not celebrated on 1 January. In fact, the date changes every year. It is based on a **lunar calendar** and each year is named after one of twelve different animals.

The Chinese Dragon Boat Festival is celebrated with boat races. The boats are in the shape of dragons. The festival usually takes place in June.

The Moon Festival happens in autumn. It is a time for family reunions. Families often get together and eat moon cakes. No one is sure of the Moon Festival's origin. One legend tells of a woman who took a pill to become a fairy and flew to the Moon to escape her cruel husband. Supposedly, she can be seen on the Moon during this festival.

▲ **CHINESE NEW YEAR**
Celebrating the New Year traditionally calls for parades, paying off debts and cleaning the house. Everyone wears red for good luck.

Learning the language

English	Chinese	How to say it
Hello	Ni Hao	(NEE-HOW)
Goodbye	Zaijian	(DZAU-JYEN)
My name is	Wo deh min zi shi	(WOO-DUH-MING-DZ-SHR)
My last name is	Wo xing	(WOOH-SHING)
Good night	Wan an	(WAHB-AHN)

Quick facts

China

Capital
Beijing

Borders
Mongolia, Russia (N)
North Korea (NE)
Pacific Ocean (E)
India, Nepal, Bhutan, Laos,
Myanmar, Vietnam (S)
Afghanistan, Pakistan (W)
Kazakhstan, Kyrgyzstan,
Tajikistan (NW)

Area
9,596,960 sq km
(3,705,392 sq miles)

Population
1,284,303,705

▼ **Geography of China**

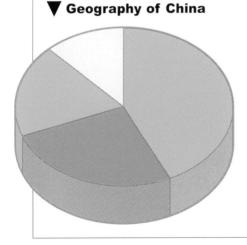

Largest cities
Shanghai (15,000,000 people)
Beijing (12,000,000 people)

Chief crops
Rice, potatoes, sorghum, peanuts

Natural resources
Coal, iron ore, crude oil,
mercury, tin

Mountain range 43%
Mountainous plateaus 26%
Basins and hilly terrain 19%
Plains 12%

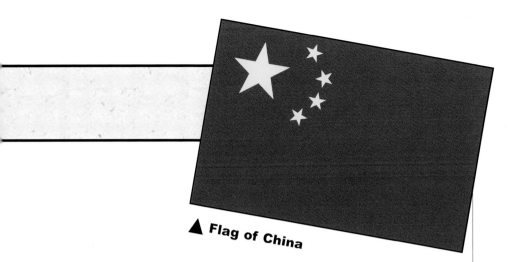

▲ Flag of China

Coastline
9010 miles (14,500 km)

Longest river ▶
Chang Jiang (Yangtze)
third-longest in the world,
6300 km (3900 miles)

Literacy rate
81.5% of all Chinese
can read.

Major industries
Iron, steel, coal

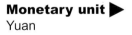

Monetary unit ▶
Yuan

People to know

Many people have made China the fascinating place that it is. Here are some to find out more about.

◄ Empress Dowager Cixi

Born in 1835, Cixi became a **concubine** to Emperor Hsien Feng. When her son, Tsai Chun, became emperor, Cixi became empress. Empress Cixi almost brought China to financial ruin. She just could not resist the finest jewellery and food.

► Mao Zedong

Mao Zedong (1893–1976) was one of the founders of the Chinese Communist Party and was the first chairman of the People's Republic of China. He directed the Cultural Revolution in which thousands of political opponents and intellectuals were persecuted. He stayed in power until his death.

◄ Gong Li

Gong Li (b. 1965) is a popular actress. She has starred in many films to international acclaim, including *Raise the Red Lantern* (1991) and *Farewell my Concubine* (1993).

More to read

Do you want to know more about China? Take a look at the books below.

Nations of the World: China, Catherine Field
    (Raintree, 2003)
Find out all about China and its people. Learn what it is really like to live there.

*20th Century Perspectives: The Rise of
Modern China,* Tony Allan (Heinemann Library, 2002)
Find out about Mao Zedong, the Cultural Revolution and how China became a Communist state.

Turning Points in History: The Long March, Tony Allan
    (Heinemann Library, 2001)
Learn about the events that led up to the Cultural Revolution and its effect on China.

Continents: Asia, L. Foster
    (Heinemann Library, 1998)
Learn about the weather, languages, animals, plants and famous places in China and other countries in Asia.

A World of Recipes: China, Julie McCulloch
    (Heinemann Library, 2001)
Find out about Chinese food and learn how to make your favourite Chinese recipes.

Glossary

Allies Great Britain, Australia, the USA and other countries that fought together in World Wars I and II

atrocity cruel act sometimes involving murder

bureaucracy many levels or departments of government working together

commerce trade of goods on a large scale between countries or individuals

communism system of government based on the theory that society should be classless and totally ruled by the state

concubine woman who lives with a man as a second or third wife, without actually being married to him

culture way of life of a society or civilization

dynasty series of rulers from the same family

economy a country's way of running its industries, trade and money

endangered at risk of dying out

ethnic group people of a particular racial group

excavation digging up land to put up a building or to look for old remains

extinct no longer in existence; all members of a group have died out

famine dangerous lack of food

fertile good for growing crops

habitat region where a plant or animal naturally lives

isolated kept separate or alone

lease agreement to give someone else use of property in return for money

lunar calendar calendar based on the Moon's cycle

monsoon strong wind that changes direction according to the season, bringing torrential rain from the sea

naval about the navy or ships

philosopher person who studies the nature of things and how the world works

pollution substances that dirty or poison the land, air and water

proletarian about the common people

province portion of a country, usually with its own local government

reform improvement in a system

renovated something old that has been repaired and made more modern

republic form of government, without a monarch, in which the people vote for their government officials

revolution forced overthrow of a government by the people

symbol sign or object that stands for something

temperate zone area of the globe with a climate that is neither too hot nor too cold

treaty formal agreement especially between countries

turmoil state of great confusion and trouble

Index